PUPPETRY

NATIONAL THEATRE BACKSTAGE GUIDES

To audiences, the work that goes on behind the scenes of a theatre can sometimes feel mysterious and the sheer number of people involved often unknown. It is often said that it takes a village to get things done and that is certainly true of theatre. At the National Theatre, writers, directors, designers and companies of actors work alongside skilled craftspeople to realize the productions audiences see on stage, from wigs, hair and make-up artists to stage management, casting, sound, lighting and video, costume and even armourers.

The National Theatre Backstage Guides series aims to bring the skills behind much of this talent to the fore, offering practical and positive introductions to different aspects of theatre-making. These guides don't presume previous knowledge about each discipline and are equally perfect for those who are merely curious to understand more about how practitioners work as well as those looking to start out in the industry or to progress.

The series celebrates the ingenuity and dedication of those involved in theatre-making, but it also aims to incite future talent. There is no one perfect route into the theatre industry and, as such, these books are not masterclasses. Written by experts, with lived examples, humour and personal insight, they reflect on changes within the industry and may challenge your assumptions about the work involved. Through practical exercises, tips and tricks to improve – or even begin – your practice, they offer a springboard for finding out more or for further development.

Other titles in the National Theatre Backstage Guides series:

Wigs, Hair and Make-Up: A Backstage Guide, by Helen Casey
Playwriting: A Backstage Guide, by Dan Rebellato
Acting: A Backstage Guide, by Lucian Msamati
Auditioning: A Backstage Guide, by Sam Stevenson

PUPPETRY

A Backstage Guide

Toby Olié

methuen | drama

LONDON • NEW YORK • OXFORD • NEW DELHI • SYDNEY

METHUEN DRAMA
Bloomsbury Publishing Plc, 50 Bedford Square, London, WC1B 3DP, UK
Bloomsbury Publishing Inc, 1359 Broadway, New York, NY 10018, USA
Bloomsbury Publishing Ireland, 29 Earlsfort Terrace, Dublin 2, D02 AY28, Ireland

BLOOMSBURY, METHUEN DRAMA and the Methuen Drama logo are trademarks of Bloomsbury Publishing Plc

First published in Great Britain 2026

Series design by Charlotte Daniels
Illustration: Elena Durey

A catalogue record for this book is available from the British Library.

A catalog record for this book is available from the Library of Congress.

ISBN: PB: 978-1-350-43745-6
ePDF: 978-1-350-43746-3
eBook: 978-1-350-43748-7

Series: National Theatre Backstage Guides

Typeset by Integra Software Services Pvt. Ltd.
Printed and bound in Great Britain

For product safety related questions contact productsafety@bloomsbury.com.

To find out more about our authors and books visit www.bloomsbury.com and sign up for our newsletters.

CONTENTS

FIGURES

FULL PRODUCTION CREDITS

© *Pinocchio* by Dennis Kelly, with songs from the Walt Disney film by Leigh Harline, Ned Washington and Paul J. Smith, adapted by Martin Lowe.

Director: John Tiffany.

Set and Costume Designer and Puppet Co-Designer: Bob Crowley.

Movement Director: Steven Hoggett.

Puppetry Director and Puppet Co-Designer: Toby Olié.

Lighting Designer: Paule Constable.

Sound Designer: Simon Baker.

Illusions: Jamie Harrison.

Music Director: Tom Brady.

PREFACE

I made my first puppet at the age of six. I was (and arguably still am) in my dinosaur phase, and my school library had a copy of Usborne's *The KnowHow Book of Puppets* which featured an egg box dinosaur puppet on the front cover. After getting the book out I remember heading home to ask my parents if we had any of the items needed to make the puppet: an egg box, woollen jumper sleeve, PVA glue and two bottle caps. The eggs were placed in some kitchen roll to keep them safe after their box was sacrificed for my needs, and while the sleeve wasn't woollen like the example, my mum very kindly donated a jersey sweatshirt to the cause. Due to some overzealous nostril glueing, the end result of my first attempt at puppet-making looked more like a hippo than the dinosaur in the book, but I loved him all the same. What this set in motion was a childhood of my family not only saving 'useful' bits of cardboard or tube for my next puppets, but them being generous and supportive when I commandeered them and my friends into puppeteering in whatever show or movie re-enactment I was performing from behind the ironing board that month.

When it came to choosing what I wanted to study at university, I sought out theatre design courses that featured puppetry modules, but in doing so I discovered a BA degree in Puppetry at The Royal Central School of Speech and Drama (now sadly discontinued). I was very excited to earn a place on the course, and be among fellow cardboard-loving puppet geeks to make shows, but found myself as the only student on the course that year. While I was disappointed at first, this ended up being a blessing, as I was put with students from the other creative disciplines to integrate puppetry into our projects, and eventually public productions. This resulted in

FIGURE 0.1 Craig Leo, Tommy Luther and Toby Olié as Joey in rehearsals for *War Horse*.
© Mervyn Millar, 2007.

me not only learning the fundamentals of collaboration, but also taking responsibility for all aspects of puppetry: from its conception as a designer/director all the way through to performance as a puppeteer.

My first professional job out of university was as a puppeteer, after Mervyn Millar, a guest tutor on my course, offered me the chance to audition for the development workshops of a show centring around a horse in the First World War that was being planned at the National Theatre. To fit a very long story into this preface, I was cast as one of the three puppeteers of Joey the horse in the original production of *War Horse* in the Olivier Theatre in 2007, and stayed with the show throughout its revival and eventual West End transfer in 2009. The show won a host of awards and changed expectations worldwide of what puppetry was capable of. But, for me personally, it demonstrated that my childhood passion could be a central storytelling element of theatre in its own right, capable of bringing an audience to tears or causing them to gasp in surprise, as well as entertaining them.

Since *War Horse* I have been very fortunate to continue to forge a career in puppetry, and more recently I have started directing and designing projects of my own. But it wasn't until the lockdowns of 2020 that I had the urge to write about puppetry. Like so many theatre-makers, I had projects postponed or cancelled entirely in the aftermath of theatres being closed, so I looked for ways to stay creative and hopefully entertain people in the process. The Little Angel

Theatre in London was commissioning puppetry artists to create short films that were released weekly online, and it was in the middle of filming mine that I had an enjoyable epiphany. I had needed a surface with adjustable height that I could position my film's cardboard theatre upon, so I got out my ironing board, only to realize that it was the exact same ironing board that I had used as a child to perform behind for my family, and had unwittingly inherited when I moved to London for university. This bizarre full-circle moment at the age of thirty-five, back to performing cardboard puppets at home, was the impetus behind the book that you are about to read, one that I hope might inspire you to raid your kitchen cupboards for 'useful' cardboard to get started yourself.

INTRODUCTION

The word *puppet* in the English language has its origins in the Latin *pupa*, meaning doll or girl, which by the fifteenth century had become *poppet* in Late Middle English. It is then believed that by the mid-sixteenth century, the use of *puppet* had come to refer to a doll or small figure that was specifically performed or animated. The origins and evidence for the first ever puppets, however, stretch much further back in time. Some 25,000 years ago in the Palaeolithic era, when early Homo sapiens carved tiny human figures from bones, stones and animal tusks. While the specific use of these figures may never be known, it is certainly the first recorded example of humans creating miniature versions of themselves. Puppets emerged out of prehistory into the ancient civilizations of Greece, Egypt and the Middle East, where figures were made from wood and terracotta and had limbs attached by thin cords for articulation. Having featured in shamanic and religious ceremonies across the globe for thousands of years, many people believe that puppetry preceded acting as a mode of performance. The history of puppets and their constantly evolving forms is a vast and rich topic in itself, one that spans countless countries and cultures – and one that would far exceed the maximum word count in this book if I tried to commit it to paper. Instead, to provide some context for the rest of the book, I will outline the definitions of some of the most familiar forms of puppet seen today. It feels important to acknowledge at this early point that nearly every contemporary form of puppet in the UK has its origins in the traditions of countries and cultures outside the Western sphere of Europe and North America. So the definitions and descriptions below are here as a means of both characterizing and recognizing the evolution of these forms over thousands of years from all over the world.

Types of puppet

String puppets or marionettes are animated by thin strings that run from the body and limbs of the puppet to a control held above by the puppeteer. A majority of the puppet's movements are created by tilting or swaying the control, but individual strings can be pulled to gesture or animate specific limbs. Some of the earliest documented examples of string puppets are from *Kathputli*, a puppet theatre native to Rajasthan, India. Believed to be over a thousand years old, the style of puppet has a single string that runs between each carved figure and their puppeteer. The more multi-stringed marionettes commonly seen in Europe and America are believed to have been fully realized in the mid-nineteenth century by a marionettist called Thomas Holden.

Rod puppets are figures traditionally operated from below, with a main rod held by the puppeteer that runs through the body and into the head. Secondary, thinner rods may also be attached to the arms or legs of the figure and operated with the puppeteer's other hand. One of the world's most renowned forms of rod puppetry is called *Wayang golek* and is native to West Java, Indonesia where it emerged in the seventeenth century and continues to tell stories of religion and myths today. In the early twentieth century, puppeteer Richard Teschner, claiming to be inspired by Javanese rod puppets he'd seen from Dutch travellers, opened his own rod puppet theatre in Vienna. His work is believed to have led to the founding of a number of puppet theatres across Europe and the United States.

Glove or hand puppets have a hollow fabric body that is worn on the puppeteer's hand. Often the puppeteer's index finger is in the puppet's head with the middle finger and thumb being in each arm, but there are other variations. *Budaixi* is a form of glove puppet opera (translated literally as 'cloth sack play') that originated in Fujian, China in the sixteenth century and retells famous legends and folklore. These puppets often have carved hands that can hold weapons and are renowned for their dexterity and acrobatics. Europe's own folklore characters Mr Punch (United Kingdom), Guignol (France), Kasper (Germany) and Pulcinella (Italy) have all appeared as satirical glove puppet shows since the seventeenth century. They are often seen as entertainment for children, but with humour and themes derived from more adult experiences.

Shadow puppets are traditionally a two-dimensional cut-out figure that is illuminated from behind, allowing its shadow to be seen by the audience on a translucent screen. They can be made from solid materials like wood, plastic or thick cardboard, and are operated on rods either from below, above or even at right angles to the screen. *Tholu bommalata* is one of the earliest forms of shadow puppetry to be documented in around the third century BCE, and comes from the state of Andhra Pradesh in India. These shadow puppets are made from leather that is perforated with intricate designs and even painted, as their decoration can be seen by the audience through the screen. *Wayang kulit* is a form of shadow puppet theatre from Java and Bali in Indonesia that is believed to have derived from *Tholu bommalata. Wayang kulit* performances occur at night and can last up to nine hours, with audience members able to watch the show from either side of the screen.

Table-top puppets emerged in European and American puppet theatre, and are called so because the puppets are usually performed on a table-height surface with their puppeteers standing behind it. Table-top puppets are usually very directly held, with only short rods or tabs, resulting in very dynamic, fluid movements. This form is widely believed to be a simplified form of Japanese *Bunraku* puppetry, first seen in the sixteenth century. In *Bunraku* three puppeteers perform a single character collectively, requiring extraordinary coordination and focus. The puppeteers aren't hidden and can be seen by the audience, and their puppets are performed without a stage surface, at waist height. The main puppeteer operates the head and one hand of the puppet, a second puppeteer operates the other hand, while the third puppeteer operates the feet.

It's fair to say that although puppets have been around for many thousands of years, over the past few decades they have had a resurgence across mainstream theatre, appearing more frequently in plays, musicals and opera. Particularly in productions where puppets perform alongside actors, having regularly been used as special effects or substitutes for animals and children, puppets now consistently play leading roles and share the stage and narrative weight with the actors around them. I was blown away when I first saw Julie Taymor's ground-breaking stage musical of *The Lion King* as a teenager. It not only combines numerous different forms of puppet and mask to portray its entirely animal cast, but also exposes its own stagecraft and mechanics in the process, resulting in the audience's imagination being complicit in bringing the characters and their narrative to life on stage. It's this form of 'suspending your disbelief' that for me makes puppetry the epitome of theatre itself, acknowledging that what you're seeing isn't reality but applying your own understanding and emotions to make it feel like a reality.

As an art form, puppetry comprises several different disciplines, and this book will give you an overview of these

FIGURE 0.2 Joe Idris-Roberts as Pinocchio, with Audrey Brisson and James Charlton as Jiminy Cricket in *Pinocchio*. Photograph © Manuel Harlan, 2017.

different strands and how they interact and respond to each other throughout the process of creating a puppet from conception all the way to its performance. A puppet is often bespoke to the needs of the production it is created for, and the result of many talented minds and hands in its design, construction and performance. To show the progression through this process I am using the puppets that I co-designed and directed for *Pinocchio* at the National Theatre in 2017 as a case study, but the same stages and methods would apply for any puppet I create. My own creative process and techniques are the product of the teachers, mentors and colleagues I have learnt from and shared skills with. Therefore, I want to say that this book is by no means a definitive guide or set of rules, as one of my favourite things about puppetry is the constant exploration and learning from project to project that may lead your ideas in a number of different directions.

1 TRAINING

How do I get into puppetry? is a frequently asked question, and the answer isn't as straightforward as I wish it could be. This is because there aren't many focused routes into puppetry in terms of training in the UK, at least not to the extent of other theatre disciplines like acting, directing, stage management or set and costume design. Many higher education institutions including the Royal Welsh College of Music and Drama and East 15 include puppetry modules as part of their undergraduate design or performance courses, and in 2023 a postgraduate course in puppetry was launched at Wimbledon College of Art. In 2016, puppetry director Sarah Wright founded the Curious School of Puppetry, an annual, eight-week intensive course for those wishing to use puppetry in their creative practice. While the limited number of full-time puppetry training opportunities might sound a bit gloomy at first, the advantage of this is that those who find themselves working in puppetry are extremely passionate and driven about what they do, and as a result are very willing to share their knowledge and experience to inspire and nurture future generations of theatre-makers.

I think this generosity also stems from the fact that, from the audience's perspective, puppetry as an art form isn't about the people but the puppets, so more often than not you encounter a shy and ego-less work ethic from even the most successful and established of artists in the industry.

Starting out

An immediate – and often unexpected – advantage of a career in puppetry is that you don't need expensive materials or equipment to begin your learning, a majority of artists working in puppetry today started out by experimenting with recycled materials or repurposed household objects to explore their potential as a puppet-maker or puppeteer. Your imagination is the most vital component, and *how* you use it, rather than *what* you use it on, is the thing that will ignite and define your abilities and practice. The first thing to consider is what aspect, or indeed aspects, of puppetry you are interested in and therefore what skills you will need to progress in the industry. Careers in puppetry can be divided up into five different disciplines: design, construction, directing, performance and maintenance. Some artists working in puppetry specialize in one of these strands, while others might work across two of the disciplines that directly correlate – design and construction, for example – and sometimes there are artists who work across three or more of these strands, instigating and implementing a majority of the creative process themselves. Often the scale and budget of a production might not allow for individual artists working in each of these disciplines, so being a bit of a multi-tasker can be helpful not only in your understanding of the wider art form, but also for your employability.

Next thing is to immerse yourself in the work of other artists working in your preferred style or discipline of puppetry: this can be any combination of live performances, remote research and online archives like Digital Theatre or National Theatre at Home. Seeing the breadth and scope of the work being created allows you to not only identify what your aspirations and passions in puppetry might be, but also begin to develop your own taste and style. If you are an aspiring designer or maker I would recommend keeping a sketchbook or regularly collating your doodles, sketches

TIP

A sketchbook doesn't always have to mean a literal, paper book. If you use drawing apps to sketch then a digital archive of material can be just as effective. Prioritize whatever gives you the most immediate means to document and access your ideas, as well as potentially share them with others.

or thinking, wherever they might occur (I'm still unable to work in a single sketchbook and regularly draw on random pieces of scrap paper). This will enable you to both reflect on and refine your abilities and ideas, as your creative process or problem solving will be merging and developing alongside your more tangible skills base.

Skills and experience

Many theatres, companies and artists run puppetry short courses or part-time training opportunities both in person or online, these are a great way to explore and enhance new skills in your preferred discipline and network with other emerging artists. The multidisciplinary nature of puppetry could also mean that some short courses, not specifically focused on puppetry, would also inform and benefit your abilities. For makers, courses in sculpture, pattern-cutting and carpentry would be very beneficial, and, for performers, skills in devising, mask and physical theatre would be invaluable. I know of professional puppeteers who have done short courses in puppet-making to improve their knowledge of puppet forms and functions, and professional puppet-makers who have done short courses in puppeteering to broaden their perspective of a puppet's movement and expression. Connecting with other artists who share your passion and finding a sense of creative community

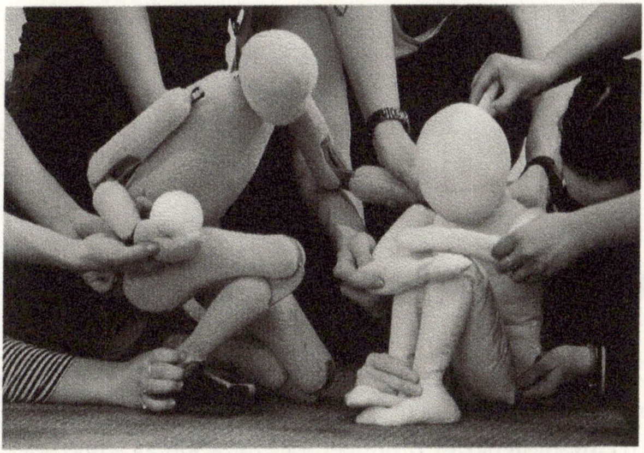

FIGURE 1.1 Neutral puppets being used as training tools.

is a valuable foundation for your creative thinking and development at this initial stage.

Work experience is a great way of witnessing creative practices in the industry first hand, and is also an invaluable means to learn new skills while building a network of professional contacts. This can take many forms, including shadowing during a rehearsal or making process, a work placement while in full-time education, or a paid internship or traineeship when starting out. These opportunities are often advertised online, but you can also enquire about any possible shadowing or placements directly to artists or companies via their websites. Often, the broader and less specific an enquiry is, the less likely you might be to get an answer, so identify what aspect of someone's practice it is that inspires you or that you want to learn more about, and mention how you and your work would benefit from seeing it first hand.

Auditions and interviews

If you are interested in a project as a designer or maker you may be asked to have an interview with either a production's director, designer or producer. Or, for a job as a puppeteer, there will most likely be an audition process led by members of the creative team – sometimes called the artistic team – and a casting director.

If a puppetry audition is for a new piece of theatre, then most likely the puppets still will be under construction and not present to be auditioned with, so either an existing puppet with similarities or perhaps more abstract materials will be used to test your abilities (my audition for *War Horse* involved a tiny piece of driftwood and a huge drinking fountain plastic bottle). The creative team and casting director will be looking at your instincts, in both listening and responding through the puppet, as well as relevant problem-solving skills like correcting a puppet's walking rhythm or action without 'stopping' it dead. Depending on the style of puppetry, auditions may be in groups or individually, if they are in groups then your ability to collaborate and contribute will be under observation. Most of the time an audition isn't about being a technically flawless puppeteer, but is about showing your enthusiasm, commitment and ability to inhabit the puppet's thoughts and actions.

For an interview it may be helpful to have some examples of your previous work to demonstrate your abilities and experience (this doesn't have to just be professional employment, things you have made at home or for amateur productions are just as beneficial if they showcase your skills effectively). Puppetry is primarily a visual medium, so a selection of sketches, photos or even videos will showcase your work effectively in a way that descriptions or anecdotes might not. If you were a part of a team working on a build or project, then be specific about which aspects of the construction or process you were responsible for, as employers might be looking for a specific skill set if they

TIP

Photos and videos showcasing your work to a potential employer don't necessarily need to feature the finished outcome. Sometimes 'in progress' documentation can be a more helpful way of demonstrating your abilities and standards of finish.

are assembling a team. There are advantages to being either a specialist or a good 'all-rounder' in terms of skills, but showing your abilities to collaborate and communicate ideas alongside your individual skills and style will often make the interviewer's decision an easy one.

Interview with Fred Davis

Fred Davis is a puppeteer who works across theatre, film and television. In 2022, he won an Olivier Award after the team of seven puppeteers responsible for Richard Parker, the tiger in *Life of Pi*, were collectively awarded for Best Actor in a Supporting Role.

TO What was your first job as a puppeteer?

FD My first job as a puppeteer also happened to be my first professional theatre job. As a child I was a member of the Chichester Festival Youth Theatre, and in 2015 they took on the challenge of adapting Michael Morpurgo's novel *Running Wild* for the stage. They brought in Finn Caldwell and yourself to create the puppetry, who gave me and the other kids involved a solid starting point in puppetry training. I found it fascinating and was hungry for more, so when I was asked to perform in a fully fledged, professional version of *Running Wild* at Regent's Park Open Air Theatre, I accepted the job and, luckily, was able to defer taking my final A-level exams. It turned out to be completely worth the upheaval – I made lifelong friends, and it's no exaggeration to say that it has led to years of consistent work since. It was a significant stepping stone into an industry that can often feel impenetrable without going to drama school. I was really lucky that *Running Wild* and other jobs early on in my career acted as a sort of training ground for me, I learned so much about how to behave on and off stage from watching my peers. I tried to be a sponge and soak up the bits of other peoples' experience and expertise, and was ultimately really fortunate to be surrounded by so many talented, hardworking and generous performers. At this point I felt really clueless (albeit with all the bravado of an eighteen-year-old), but the more time I've spent working as a performer, the more I realize the extent to which we're all constantly learning and growing – the training never stops!

TO How do you go about getting future work?

FD The puppetry world is so small and tight knit, it often seems like everyone either knows each other or has a handful of mutual friends, so you are often aware of current or upcoming projects. I'm lucky enough to have friends who create their own work, and find myself working on their projects at the development stage, trying to help make their vision a reality. Being involved in these early stages means that if the project goes on to have a future life, I am already known to the creative team and therefore have a good chance of being considered in the casting process. It's also worth mentioning that I don't have an agent, so I try to keep an ear to the ground for upcoming projects that might interest me, and make myself known to the casting team involved. Sending introductory emails can feel strange and impersonal, but I have found it to be a necessary way of connecting with people and finding new work. As long as you're professional, unapologetic and don't pester people, it's rare that anyone would react badly. I bear more responsibility for this kind of self-promotion than someone with an agent, but, in an industry that is so reliant on personal connections, it works for me. Of course, once you've made those connections and secured a job, by doing the job well you are giving people a reason to keep employing you. In my experience, it seems to be just as important to be nice as it is to be skilled – maybe even more important.

TO What are the best and worst aspects of being a puppeteer?

FD One of the best parts of being a puppeteer has to be when the team I'm in gets to the point that we can fully communicate without talking. Once we know the character inside and out, we know the story and we start to add minute detail to the blocking that is so subtle it's almost meant to be missed. It's those tiny details that allow us to bring the inanimate object we're holding to life in a realistic way. It feels like magic, but a type of magic where the audience already knows how the trick is done and are still mesmerized regardless. It's a sense of teamwork and unity unlike any other, and a feeling that I'm always chasing.

One of the worst things about being a puppeteer is that it's easy for people to underestimate what is required of us physically. Puppetry can take a huge toll on the body and requires a high level of self-care to try and avoid injury. It's a constant battle to drink enough water and get enough sleep whilst keeping up with strength and flexibility training, in addition to helpful things like ice baths, saunas, supplements for muscle recovery and, of course, a lot of physiotherapy. I think part of the reason people don't always realize this is because a large part of a puppeteer's job is for the puppetry to look effortless and therefore go unnoticed. However, it can mean that these important methods of physical maintenance aren't always factored into the process of creating and performing a show.

TO What advice would you give someone wanting to start a career in puppetry?

FD I find it hard to give advice when I feel I've got so much still to learn, but here are a few bits of advice that I've picked up in the last few years:

Familiarize yourself with the puppet as best you can. Learning how a puppet has been made to move makes it easier to find the most economical ways of getting the performance you want. Initially, it can seem like a different handle position or new mechanism will solve your problems, but, most of the time, what is actually needed is just to spend a bit more time getting to know that particular puppet's idiosyncrasies. That way it starts to feel like an extension of your body rather than a tool.

There's also no shame in not being ready. Let the relevant people know that you need more time or support instead of rushing into a show unprepared. In some scenarios, it could be dangerous not to do so, and it's never worth potentially injuring yourself or other people.

Constructive criticism and notes from an outside eye on the creative team are absolute gold dust and should be relished, not avoided. It's not personal, at least it shouldn't be, and it's all to make you, the team and the show better in the long run. It's also worth maintaining a good level of core strength and stability between jobs. The rehearsal process will usually prepare you physically for the show but having a good base level to work from is very helpful.

Finally, I think the biggest piece of advice I can give is to be a team player. When creating a show or looking for ways to improve once it's up and running, it's important to give each other grace and support, and trust that everyone has the same goal. If you're all aiming to tell the story in the best and most effective way, you can't go far wrong.

2 RESEARCH AND DEVELOPMENT

When I first graduated from my university course in 2006, I would be approached about creating puppetry for a production, on average, around two or three months before the start of the rehearsal process, which allowed for a decent amount of design and making time, providing the show doesn't have multiple puppets or large-scale characters that might require extra time. However, in recent years, with the influx of puppetry on stages across the world, I have seen a dramatic increase in the lead time up to projects, which can be anything from nine months to two years. I think this is due to the fact that directors and producers have identified that the time required to create puppetry for a production is not only about the making of the objects required, but about its conceptual devising and integration into the production alongside the other theatrical mediums. This pre-rehearsal time, when the devising and integration takes place, is often called 'workshops' or 'R&D' (research and development). At the National Theatre there is a whole separate building

FIGURE 2.1 Puppetry development workshop for *Pinocchio* with performers Tina Koch, John Leader, Avye Leventis and Charlotte Mooney.
© Toby Olié, 2016.

dedicated to the development of new productions, called the National Theatre Studio.

This is where we workshopped *War Horse* using Handspring Puppet Company's prototype horse puppets and a draft script, long before the show had even been officially commissioned. These workshops are an extremely liberating and playful period for a production team, as you create and explore ideas without the pressure to create a finished performance that an audience will see. Since *War Horse*, I have workshopped the puppetry for numerous other National Theatre productions at the studio, including: *The Light Princess*, *The Elephantom*, *Peter Pan* and *Pinocchio*.

Creating a concept

There are no fixed rules when it comes to how puppets are integrated into a production, particularly when appearing as characters opposite actors, but, for the puppets to feel like they 'belong' on stage, the production's overall design and staging concept has to make them feel like part of the world and not an afterthought. For me, the most direct way of achieving this isn't to think about the puppets, but about their puppeteers: *Who are the people that have permission to not be there?* In film, special effects departments use blue- or green-screen techniques to digitally remove puppeteers, but in theatre it has become more common to declare the puppeteers to the audience rather than hide them using costume or lighting. Visible puppeteers can use their own focus on their puppet to render themselves 'invisible' to the audience (more on this in Chapter 5), but aesthetically there's no denying that puppets have a certain amount of 'visual baggage' that comes with them, particularly if one puppet requires multiple operators to appear alive. So often the design and colour of the puppeteers' costumes not only acts as a canvas for which the puppet is 'read' against, but also incorporates the puppeteer into the production's setting and aesthetic. Some interesting examples of this are:

- *The Elephantom*: the set was a domestic room interior where every surface finish and texture of the walls and floor were purple, so we dressed our puppeteers in outfits that were sourced or dyed in matching shades of purple to almost camouflage them with their surrounding environment.
- *Peter Pan*: the production started with the Darling children playing a game of pirates before bedtime while wearing their pyjamas, and this sense of a child's imagination was the conceptual foundation of the show. The storytelling ensemble (who would also puppeteer) wore matching pyjamas to unify them and continue the theme of play and make believe once the children left their nursery for Neverland.
- *Pinocchio*: Geppetto's workshop formed the basis of the show's design, with a floor constructed from mismatched wooden boards, using giant ladders and tools to create elements like mountains and an enormous whale. The puppeteers were dressed in

FIGURE 2.2 Mark Hadfield, Stuart Angell, Michael Taibi and Scarlet Wilderink as Geppetto with Joe Idris-Roberts as Pinocchio in *Pinocchio*.
Photograph © Manuel Harlan, 2017.

paint-splattered overalls and aprons, to give them the appearance of workshop workers or assistants, there to help facilitate the needs of the world.

Whatever the treatment of the puppeteers in a production, it is always important to think about how their presence is to emphasize or prioritize the puppet's presence and performance for the audience. This kind of declared but omnipresent performer often bleeds into the way that other elements of the show are handled or staged, where the ensemble are used to change and animate scenery or step in and out of different roles on stage with a simple prop or costume change.

FACT

The Light Princess was a musical about Althea, a princess without gravity who floats mid-air. To achieve this effect on stage, Rosalie Craig, the actress performing the role of Althea, was 'puppeteered' by a troupe of four performers to give her a weightless, buoyant quality while being dressed like mysterious shadows.

Initial ideas

When it comes to creating the actual puppets for a production, there are many different practicalities to consider, like: How many performers are available to animate your puppet character? What is the character's action? Does it talk? Does it have to pick up or carry props? All of these factors will need to be considered as they have an impact on the puppet's design, construction, movement and overall performance. Sometimes these practicalities are known at the start of the process and can influence initial thinking, but very often they aren't decided yet and so the parameters can shift and respond to what the puppet needs to give its best performance. I find it helpful at this early stage to be mindful of practicalities but not dictated to by them, as often the most playful or simple idea can have the broadest scope of possibilities. I make a point of documenting every initial idea or thought that comes to mind when I first read the source material of a project, whether that is an early draft of a script, a book that is to be adapted, or perhaps even a film that will become a stage production. This usually occurs in my sketchbook and looks like a very rough, doodled, stream of consciousness. Whenever I look back at these pages at the end of a project, I'm always amazed to see either the early roots of certain ideas or, indeed, that some ideas have stayed the course and made it all the way to the finished show.

From here it is useful to research around the specific species or subject matter of your puppet, you may well even want to research different types of puppet to decipher if a particular form or scale would work best to portray your character. Whatever the subject of your research it is important to get a wide range of information and perspective

FIGURE 2.3 Initial design ideas for Sammy the Border Collie from *Goodnight Mister Tom.*
© Toby Olié, 2011.

on it, these can be images, videos or even written research, as you'll want to know as much about your subject before you create a theatrical interpretation of it. At this early stage of the process, the director and set/costume designer may also want to see and feed back on your initial ideas before the designs are generated. Therefore, a selection of visual research about your subject matter or the aesthetic direction is a very helpful way to share insight into your early thinking.

EXERCISE: ANIMAL ANALYSIS

Choose an animal to research for a puppet design, then find a combination of images from primary sources (photos of the animal in reality or its skeleton and anatomy) and secondary sources (how the animal has been interpreted in fine art, sculpture, illustration and graphic design). Analyse the images and look for common links between them with regards to the animal's form, colour, texture and behaviour. Arrange and consolidate the images (either by attaching them to large pieces of paper, or photographing them in place) to create mood boards that embody the foundations of your thinking and can showcase it to others.

Making a prototype

I am a firm believer that you can't design a puppet solely on paper, as it is impossible to anticipate how certain materials or structures will behave when animated in three dimensions. So, before the more formal design process starts, it can be beneficial to make a prototype inspired by any initial ideas, so that you start to think about form and movement, otherwise it is easy to get immersed in theorizing on a page. A prototype puppet is an initial 'tester', meaning that you are making the prototype knowing that it is a learning tool and not an item that has to function perfectly or indeed be used in the final performance. Some useful things to think about when building your prototype are:

- **Puppeteers:** How many performers will your puppet require to become alive?
- **Control points:** Where and how will the puppeteer/s hold the puppet?
- **Joints:** What kinds of joints does your puppet need? E.g. hinged, like elbows and knees, or multi-directional, like wrists and shoulders.
- **Flexibility:** Which parts of the puppet need mobility and which should stay solid?
- **Movement:** Are there any parts of the puppet that will move freely without being animated? E.g. tail, ears or hair.

It may well be that you make more than one prototype puppet as your ideas develop or consolidate, the more you hone and refine the structure and movement of your puppet in prototype form the less you will have to amend or alter the finished product. Because it is a temporary learning tool, I always strive to make prototypes out of reclaimed or recycled materials, so that it can be disposed of with a reduced environmental impact. Old cardboard boxes, packaging tubes, plastic food packaging and scrap bits of foam or fabric are perfect to use in the creation of this trial puppet. Recently,

I have been trialling another means of limiting waste at this early stage, by making prototypes with the idea that they could be dismantled after use into separate components that could be repurposed into future prototypes. This could be as simple as salvaging the rods and handles for use on an entirely different puppet, or more innovative like making the prototype's limbs adjustable in length so that the puppet could be transformed for use in another creative process.

For *Pinocchio*, we made a series of evolving prototype puppets during three development workshops over a period of eighteen months. Initially these were purely to explore and define the scale and articulation of the oversized human puppets that would play Geppetto and the other adult characters in the production. But eventually the character of Jiminy Cricket came up as something the creative team wanted to explore, whether she should be played by an actor, an assembly of everyday objects or a puppet. Determined for the character to be a puppet, I set about creating a prototype puppet with puppet supervisor Daisy Beattie as a means of practically demonstrating the expressive possibilities and comedic capabilities of a puppet in the role. We repurposed some arms from an old puppet and combined this with a carved foam head, some cardboard legs and an upturned plastic bleach bottle for the body. These simple materials meant that in the workshop we could easily adjust or alter the puppet in response to the requirements of the script and staging. Noticeable changes included lengthening the arm rods so the puppeteer could pass them under Jiminy mid

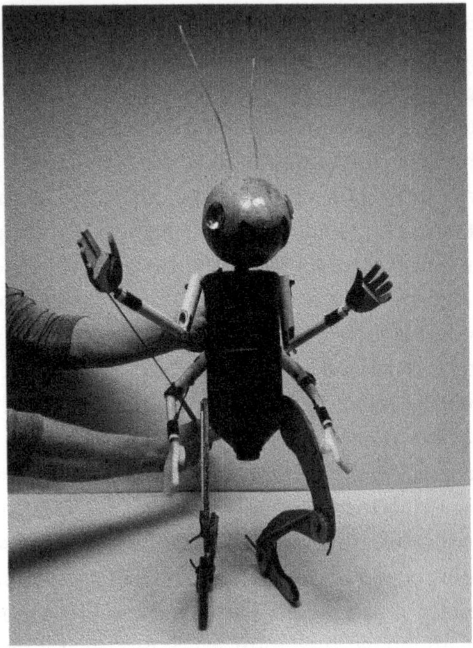

FIGURE 2.4 The prototype puppet of Jiminy Cricket from *Pinocchio*.
© Toby Olié, 2016.

jump while still holding on, and using elastic in her knee and ankle joints so her legs could still compress and straighten even when there wasn't a second puppeteer directly animating them. I was overjoyed when the puppet proved so expressive that the other ideas of an actor or objects weren't even tried in the workshop. Jiminy had evolved and continued to deliver an affecting performance through the various challenges the puppet was put through, and to this day she remains one of my favourite creations.

FACT

The original prototype puppet of Joey in *War Horse* was created to be operated by just two puppeteers inside the horse's body. However, during development workshops, it was soon determined that Joey's head needed to be constantly animated, so a temporary rod was attached and a third puppeteer added.

3 DESIGN

Now that you have explored your puppet in three dimensions and have a sense of its movements, it is time to think about what your puppet will look like aesthetically, and what its appearance will communicate to the audience. You might be wondering why I don't start the process by defining the appearance of the puppet before prototyping and thinking about its movement? My reasoning behind this comes from some advice I received from puppet designer and maker Peter O'Rourke, who was a project mentor while I was training. Peter said I should never sacrifice a puppet's movement for its aesthetic, as the way a puppet moves is its primary form of expression for the audience. Because puppets are representations or symbols of reality, and the audience are complicit in bringing them to life with their own imaginations, the puppet's appearance is very definitive, whereas its movements are more suggestive. For example, a scrunched up piece of paper is a very abstract puppet upon first glance, but animate it to have an enthusiastic energy and a wagging rear end and it could easily suggest a dog. However, a fully realized dog puppet is very much a dog to an audience, and very little else. Yes, it can do non-naturalistic things like fly or talk with the help of its puppeteers, but in the audience's eyes it will always appear to be a dog. Granted you might want your puppet to be more literal than scrunched paper, but always look for ways that form combined with movement can *suggest* instead of *show*.

While I was designing the puppets for *The Elephantom*, we knew we needed a flexible and playful trunk for the ghost elephant that would be the sole responsibility of one puppeteer to animate. Our prototype trunk was made of foam discs around a fabric core, which was very effective, yet when we went to cover the trunk in a flexible lycra skin to hide the gaps between the discs, the fabric significantly reduced its movement. The solution? Not to cover the trunk and keep the discs exposed, but change the width of the discs so that the gaps suggested deep wrinkles in the trunk. The quality of the more stylized trunk's movement won out over the solidity of a more naturalistic-looking

FACT

The Elephantom was a play combining actors and an enormous ghost elephant puppet. Due to a lack of wing space in the theatre, the puppet had an entirely inflatable body to allow it to 'disappear' offstage without blocking the backstage area.

trunk, and the fact it engaged the audience even more is a huge benefit to their enjoyment of the cheeky elephant's action.

Artwork

When creating designs for a puppet, whether this is on paper or digitally, it is important to think about the audience for the artwork. You will often find yourself having to explain your designs to different collaborators or departments throughout the creative process, which means creating different kinds of artwork. For me this breaks down into two categories:

- **Conceptual**: a design that shows how the puppet finished puppet will look on stage to the audience.
- **Anatomical**: a design that shows the puppet's internal structures and joint construction.

A director, set/costume designer and lighting designer will want to see the puppet's overall aesthetic to determine how it will correlate with everything else on stage, so a conceptual drawing gives them that perspective. Whereas, the puppet-makers, props department and stage management or puppet technician will need to see its construction and how it functions for either its creation or repair, so something more anatomical illustrates that information.

FIGURE 3.1 Conceptual artwork for Jiminy Cricket from *Pinocchio*.

For conceptual artwork, I always include the puppeteers in my drawings, often just in simple silhouette form, as this not only provides a sense of the puppet's scale, but also shows how many puppeteers it requires and their proximity around or behind the character. Other members of the creative team will also benefit from being reminded of the presence of the puppeteers, as we tend to think about the finished result that the audience will see with 'invisible' manipulators. So, acknowledging their presence in the artwork helps provide a basis for continued conversations about their costume design,

FIGURE 3.2 Anatomical artwork for Jiminy Cricket from *Pinocchio*.
© Toby Olié, 2017.

or how the lighting designer might light the character. I am a big fan of using watercolour paints for conceptual designs as it is easy to build up depth or layers of colour and then you can work in over the top of them with pencil or pen to create greater definition. Another technique I use is collage, cutting the different elements of the design out of printed photographs of objects or materials to give the design more depth and texture.

The clearest way to create an anatomical artwork is by drawing the front and side profiles of the puppet next to one another. I first saw this technique when I visited the Little

Angel Theatre, London, and met its co-founder Lyndie Wright, who works in its adjoining workshop. Lyndie will always draw the aligned profiles of the puppet as a way of identifying the overall shapes and forms of the puppet. It doesn't matter which profile you choose to draw first, one might seem more straightforward than the other, but be sure to use horizontal lines from one profile to the other to ensure the body parts and joints are all aligned properly. You can then use tracing paper or photocopies of the puppet to replicate its limbs and place them on top to identify the pivot points of any joints or mechanisms (more on mechanisms in Chapter 4). These anatomical drawings then become the blueprints for your puppet, not only aiding in its construction but also providing value insight into how it functions should it need repairing – they're also invaluable should you ever need to replicate your puppet.

Making a maquette

In puppetry, if your final character is very large it can often be helpful to create a small-scale practice model of your puppet – often called a maquette – to practically solve elements of its design while saving the time and resources it would take to solve at full scale. This process is similar to the prototype outlined in Chapter 2, but often more specific in shape, form or articulation now that the design is more refined. One thing to consider when making maquettes is how materials move or flex at a smaller scale that may not behave in the same way once scaled up. For example, a small piece of cotton used on a maquette wing will be quite rigid compared to the flowing, full-length of cloth that the actual wing will require. So, often it is necessary to substitute materials on a maquette to get the desired effect in miniature, but make sure you explain to anyone using the maquette how the finished thing will vary from this example.

TIP

If your maquette is representing a very large puppet, then it might be helpful to build it in relation to an existing scale of human figures or homemade cut-outs. You will then be able to include these human figures alongside the maquette and showcase its ultimate scale alongside demonstrating its form and function.

4 CONSTRUCTION

If the puppet designer isn't making their own puppet, then this is the stage when a puppet-maker – or makers, depending on the size of the project – are engaged. If the show has a large amount of puppets then a puppet supervisor may also join the process, they are responsible for costing the puppet build, buying materials and coordinating the puppet-makers (more about this role later in the chapter). If the project has a team of makers, then the puppet designer and supervisor will delegate out the making tasks according to a specific maker's skill set or experience. Sometimes, a team of makers may work in parallel on separate tasks, or they might work collectively to see one section of the build through to completion, it depends entirely on the requirements of the puppet being made.

Whether I'm making the puppet or working with a supervisor and makers, construction is the most exciting and daunting part of the process. It's exciting because you start to see the ideas that have existed on paper or in prototype form come to fully realized life, but daunting because each decision you now make will have an impact on the object and ultimately affect both its performance and the puppeteers. Because of this, it is important to prioritize three factors throughout construction to ensure your puppet's performance will be the best it can be:

- **Weight:** ensuring your choice of materials or finishing keeps the puppet as lightweight as possible. It shouldn't be too much effort for the puppeteers to make the puppet simply exist in neutral on stage.
- **Ergonomics:** similar to weight, you want to make the puppet's manipulation points – rods, handles or triggers – comfortable and instinctive for the puppeteers to use.
- **Durability:** whether your show has a short run of performances or is running for years, your puppet will need to withstand a lot of use. Choose materials and outer finishes that are strong and hard wearing.

If you are mindful of these factors and keep checking in on them throughout the making process, then you will maximize the puppet's functionality and therefore its performance/acting potential throughout rehearsals and in performance. The build should in theory be the most methodical or 'press and go' part of creating a puppet, but there are so many possibilities and variables when beginning construction of a puppet, particularly in terms of materials selection and sometimes what order to make elements of it in. Often, it can be helpful to let the size and intended articulation of the character inform your decision-making about what the most suitable materials and starting points for the process are. Balance this with keeping a sense of exploration during the making process, as it can be very liberating to be steered by new discoveries and methods or even techniques used by other makers in the group.

> **TIP**
>
> Wooden dowel makes excellent handles for puppet control rods; however, its rounded shape can sometimes cause muscle fatigue through a puppeteer overgripping. Lightly sand two opposite sides of the dowel to make it a faintly square, ridged shape, this will make the handle much easier to grip and manipulate.

External forms

Using the anatomical design drawing's front and side profiles of the puppet, you can identify how many different elements of body and limb will make up the whole character, and where the joints and control points are. From here it is worth thinking about whether your puppet's external form is something that is carved away from a material like reticulated foam, polystyrene or wood; built or assembled in a material like papier-mâché, plastazote foam or thermoplastic; or even sculpted to allow for a mould to be taken and the final structure to be cast from it. It may be that your puppet needs to be hollow to reduce its weight or allow access to the maintenance of any mechanisms, or perhaps a more solid, carved form would provide stability for an active performance. Getting the puppet's bulk into a three-dimensional, full-scale reality is a big step and one that can often lead to a lot of waste as materials are carved away or cut into for pattern pieces, so be sure to retain any scraps or off-cuts of materials as they might be useful in the rest of the build, or indeed for future puppet-making and prototyping.

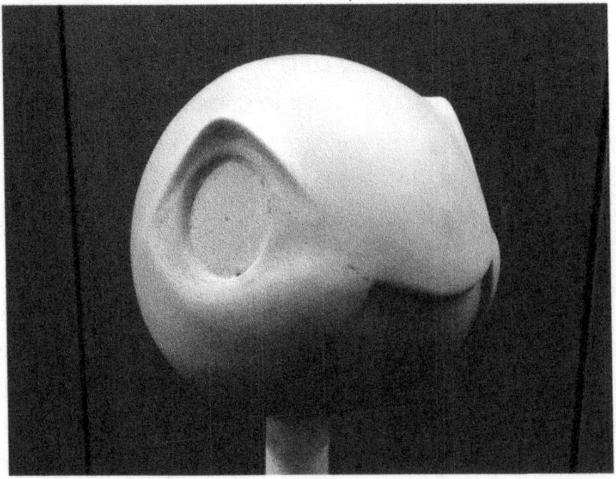

FIGURE 4.1 The finished fibreglass form of Jiminy Cricket's head.
© Toby Olié, 2017.

In the construction of Jiminy Cricket, we knew we wanted a smooth finish that would evoke the shell-like texture of an insect's exoskeleton, plus her two pairs of arms meant that certain elements would need to be identical. So we made the decision to have all of her separate sections sculpted in styrofoam and then have moulds made so that the cast shapes would be sleek and easy to replicate. Jiminy's head and body were the largest shapes and both needed to be hollow for a tilt mechanism inside the head, and access to the central control rod inside her chest. Fibreglass was deemed the best way of building up these shapes inside the moulds, but doing as few layers as possible to minimize the weight of the finished thing. Jiminy's limbs, however, were a lot finer and thinner so needed to be solid to avoid breaks. However, when we cast a few samples of them in a sturdy polyurethane resin, they were heavy, and so the collective weight of all six limbs would be too much for the puppeteer to carry with one arm. So we added a material called Glass Bubbles into the resin, these tiny, hollow particles filled the centre of the moulded form and created a hollow, honeycomb-like texture that significantly reduced the weight.

Internal structure

The inside of a puppet can be as simple as profile shapes in lightweight plywood or ribs of dense foam to reinforce and maintain the external form, but an important thing to think about is how the puppeteer's control points relate to this internal structure. The points at which handles or rods attach to the puppet get put under a lot of strain during its animation and performance, and cause damage to the puppet if they warp, and move. So these control points should extend into the puppet and attach to a solid or reinforced structure, or said structure can protrude out of the puppet and have a handle or similar attached to it. The more direct and connected a puppeteer can be to the centre of a puppet (both its form and weight), the more balanced

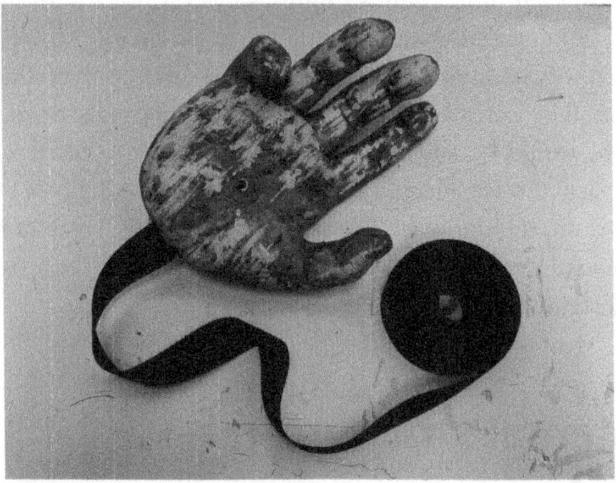

FIGURE 4.2 A length of webbing running into the Geppetto puppet's hand for *Pinocchio*.
© Toby Olié, 2017.

and rooted they will feel operating it, and thus deliver a more fluid, effective performance.

Geppetto and the other large puppet characters in *Pinocchio* were built to be as expressive and dexterous as real humans, and with teams of four puppeteers per character the stresses and strains would be applied to the puppet in all directions. So extra measures and precautions were taken to ensure their strength and flexibility. We used thick nylon webbing (the kind of material used for backpack straps) for the joints in the arms, as it is hard wearing and allows for twist and flex. But rather than use three separate sections of webbing for the shoulder, elbow and wrist joints, we ran a single long length of webbing through the entire arm. The webbing was attached to a plywood former in the body, on which the chest puppeteer's control rod was attached, it then extended out at the shoulder, through the arm, into the hand and ended with a reinforced hole through its centre so the arm puppeteer's hand rod could be attached through it. This way the arm and chest puppeteers were in direct contact and tension with each other through the webbing, rather than having shorter sections of it that might have put strain on the lightweight, sculpted sections of puppet running between them.

Mechanisms

A mechanism is a movement function on a puppet that is controlled via a trigger, ring-pull, lever or similar. Some common mechanisms include eye blink, mouth opening and head tilt. It's possible for a puppet to have multiple mechanisms, while another may have none at all, depending on the performance style or mode of operating. Mechanisms usually operate through tension, with the puppeteer pulling on a string that works in opposition to an elastic cord. For example, a mouth-opening mechanism would have an elastic inside the mouth keeping it closed when the puppet is at rest. Then a string would run from the lower jaw of the puppet to a trigger, which when pressed would pull on the string and elastic together, opening the mouth. Once the tension on the trigger is released, the elastic pulls the mouth closed. The use of tension in the mechanism means the puppeteer only performs half of the movement, then, by releasing it, the stretched elastic returning to its original length completes the action.

From experience, I find mechanisms work best when used to heighten a character's senses or emotions (ear flick, tail swish, eyebrow raise) rather than to animate actions like walking or turning their head. This is because these bigger, basic bodily actions have a myriad of rhythms and intentions that can communicate different emotions, and if you mechanize them you reduce the potential for variation or indeed imperfection, resulting in the puppet appearing robotic and repetitive instead of fluid and organic.

In *Pinocchio*, we had very few mechanisms in any of the puppets, mainly due to the fact each puppet had multiple operators so their limbs and physical expression were well

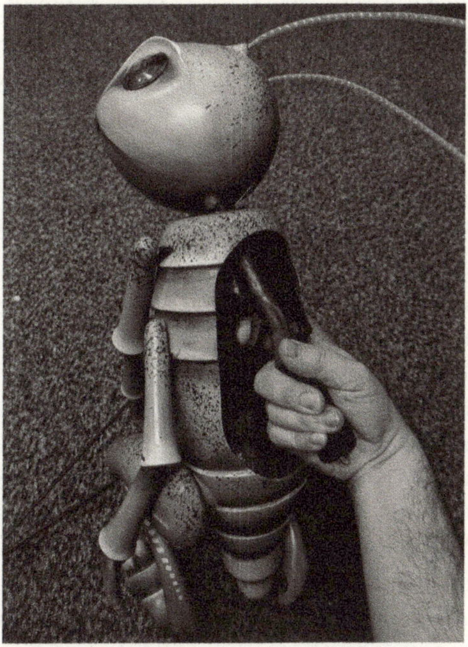

FIGURE 4.3 Jiminy Cricket's head tilt mechanism built into the head's control rod.

catered for. But the few mechanisms we did have were created to reduce the strain on the puppeteers' bodies. During the show, the larger human puppets spent a lot of time looking down at the actor playing Pinocchio, and tiny Jiminy Cricket spent a lot of time on the ground looking up at Pinocchio, so we used a head tilt mechanism on triggers (tilting down for the humans, tilting up for Jiminy) to enable the puppets to look in these directions without impacting the puppeteer's wrists, arms and backs.

Covering and finishing

Different materials require different treatments to reinforce their outermost surface and enable them to be finished as required. Solid materials like wood and polystyrene benefit from layers of brown paper and PVA glue to form a smooth but tough outer layer which can be painted or have things stuck to it. Whereas more flexible materials like foams or plastics benefit from scrimming, a process where you cover the surface in an open-weave muslin fabric using Flexbond or liquid rubbers.

The outer surface of your puppet will be handled and also make contact with other performers and props on stage, so ensuring any paints or glazes are sealed is important to avoid them scratching or leaving marks. I am a big fan of matt varnishes, as anything with a gloss or satin finish tends to make puppets look like shiny plastic toys and therefore lose a sense of their reality.

We wanted the large human puppets in *Pinocchio* to look like they were carved from wood, evoking ancient Italian religious carvings, but using wood to make a puppet at their

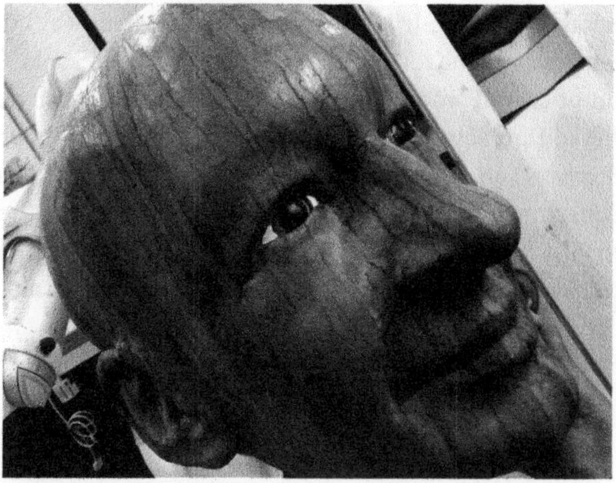

FIGURE 4.4 A wood grain effect on the *Pinocchio* puppets using brown paper.
© Toby Olié, 2017.

huge scale would have been far too heavy and cumbersome to manipulate, even for a team of puppeteers. To keep them lightweight we used a combination of polystyrene and plastazote forms to create their heads, bodies and arms. But once carved, none of these materials resembled wood, and the polystyrene in particular would be very vulnerable to chipping and denting. We began experimenting with different techniques to find a way of reinforcing the puppets, while still looking like wood. Having used brown paper and PVA glue as a puppet's outer layer a number of times in previous builds, we trialled a number of different ways that the paper could be torn and glued in alignment to evoke the grain of carved wood. The final result was very effective, it didn't add any significant weight to the already sizable puppet and created an ideal surface for finishing paint effects and the attachment of their wigs, facial hair and hats. Sometimes even just varying the application or treatment of familiar materials and processes can give you very different results.

EXERCISE: BROWN PAPER TECHNIQUE

To create a smooth and even surface, start by tearing some brown paper into small pieces (don't use scissors to cut it, as frayed, torn edges will blend better) then soak these pieces in a shallow bowl of cold water to soften them. Brush your unfinished surface in a thin layer of PVA glue, then apply your soaked pieces of paper (draining off any excess water) and secure them with another thin layer of glue over the top. Ensure you have good overlap between the pieces to create a solid layer once dry, multiple layers of paper can be added to create an extra sturdy finish.

Asking for help

If you're working as a maker as part of a bigger team and are unsure about a technique or use of a material, I would encourage you to ask the puppet designer, supervisor or lead maker for help or instruction. As even very fundamental techniques like scrimming or brown papering have subtle variations and each maker or team of makers will have their preferences, plus it may be a chance for you to learn a new method of something. Don't feel embarrassed by asking for clarification or even admitting that you're not as experienced in a technique or task that you've been delegated. Puppet-makers are always learning from each other and sharing experience on projects, so it is far better to see moments of uncertainty as a chance to learn than feel underqualified. Besides, the main cost of puppets is their making hours, so it's even better for the budget if you ask for assistance than attempt something which is either unusable or has to be taken apart to start again.

FACT

Handspring Puppet Company made a total of nine sets of puppets for the different productions of *War Horse* worldwide. A team of twenty-seven puppet-makers worked across two factory premises in Cape Town, South Africa to create them.

Interview with Daisy Beattie

Daisy Beattie's work in puppetry spans across designing, making, supervising and puppeteering. Her puppets have been seen on stages across the UK, and on screen she has puppeteered in the *Star Wars* and *Jurassic World* film franchises.

TO How do you train to be a puppet-maker?

DB I grew up among puppetry, my mum is a puppeteer and from just a few months old I regularly went to the Little Angel Theatre and Puppet Theatre Barge in north London where my mum was working. In fact, when I was a little older and mum couldn't find childcare, she used to take me to rehearsals, where I would watch the puppets come to life from the back of the auditorium in my favourite seat. Growing up I didn't immediately find my passion in puppet-making, I was unsure about what I wanted to do but knew vaguely it was something creative. The 'Design in Theatre' university course I took was disappointing, so I was left feeling confused about what direction I wanted to take. So, when I was looking for work experience in creative industries, the theatres from my childhood felt like the perfect place to start.

I ended up volunteering on Mike Sheperd's production of *A Very Old Man with Enormous Wings* at the Little Angel Theatre, shadowing Lyndie Wright, a master puppet-maker and one of the theatre's founders. I have learned so much from her over the years, and I often rent making space in her workshop to this day, where she continues to teach me. While I was volunteering I asked Lyndie about what skills she used most in puppet-making. Armed with this information, I booked myself onto short, skills-based courses: carving, clothes making, mould making and even welding. This gave me a good foundation to continue applying for junior puppet-making jobs. Then it was all about learning on the job. I made sure to watch, listen and learn in every studio and workshop that I was able to work in. Puppet-making is both a rich tradition stretching back to ancient times, and an ever evolving art form, which combines so many skills and processes. So I'll never be finished learning, there's still so much to learn.

TO What are the responsibilities of a puppet supervisor?

DB A puppet supervisor's job can differ slightly depending on needs of the production or the staffing of the theatre. But generally being a puppet supervisor will include some or all of the following:

- Initial design meetings with the puppet designer to build a foundation of understanding of what will be required for the show.
- Creating a budget for the whole of the puppet build based on puppet designs inclusive of materials and all making hours.
- Setting a build schedule and booking puppet-makers accordingly.

- Sourcing and buying all materials needed for the build.
- Managing the workshop job delegation and answering questions throughout the build to make sure the designer's vision is being realized.
- Keeping track of time sheets, invoices and accounts.
- Liaising with other heads of department, like costume and props, regarding any crossover items with puppets.

As a supervisor, I do also make the puppets alongside all of the above, but how much I make is dictated by the scale of the production. When I'm supervising a really big workshop of makers, such as the 2022 UK tour of *Animal Farm* where we had over fifty different animal puppets to build, there's too much supervision of others for me to have space to make something on my own. So, in those kinds of situations, I just have to channel my work through the multiple arms of the making team, like one big supervisory octopus.

TO What are the challenges when creating puppets for theatre?

DB One of the biggest challenges is creating something that will be sturdy enough to last through rehearsals and a whole run of shows, but also light enough to puppeteer fluidly and without putting strain on the puppeteer. Strong materials tend to be heavier, whereas the light ones tend to be more brittle or crushable, so it's often a balance of using the lighter material with reinforcements in the right places. But I love problem-solving these kinds of technical challenges.

Another challenge can be deciding which part of the puppet should be animated to best give it life and character, and what can be left to the audience's imagination. For instance, during *Pinocchio* rehearsals we had a trial audience visit with whom we shared scenes from the show. One of the comments we received was about how amazing it was that the puppets all had moving eyes and were able to blink and track across the stage. However, none of the puppets actually had moving eyes, just small, faceted buttons for pupils that catch and reflect light. The choice not to give them moving eyes didn't take away from the animation and expression of the puppet, it meant that the audience were able to see the reflected light and to project their emotion and imagination onto it. The challenge lies in creating a facial expression or a hand pose that encapsulates what could be the beginning of a number of emotions that a character might express. A bright eye can communicate laughter, or could show tears, and an open palm hand might also look like it can point or reach out to grasp something.

TO What is your relationship to the performers in a production?

DB As puppet supervisor, my role is to introduce the puppets to the performers with the director, listen to their feedback, and, if possible, adapt the puppets to get the best performance out of them. This might be as simple as tightening an elastic bungee cord, or as complex as fundamentally changing the structure of the puppet so it works in a different way.

Boxer, the shire horse from *Animal Farm*, was animated by three performers, two of whom were inside wearing backpacks. However, the pairs of performers that were inside changed throughout the show, and the performers were very different in height. So if we didn't do something, the taller performers would have to squat to avoid the horse rearing up or bend forward like a wheelbarrow. So we created a sliding system for the backpacks using aluminium square tubing and clevis pins, that allowed them to be adjusted and repositioned during the show. How many changes are possible is dependent on how much time there is available and how necessary the change is for the show. Of course, we always aim to get it right the first time, but, since most things we make are new, bespoke designs, and we try to push the boundaries of what's possible, this is much easier said than done.

TO What advice would you give emerging/aspiring puppet-makers?

DB If I was a young adult wanting to get involved in puppetry, I would watch as many shows as possible, get as much experience as possible, and write to practitioners I like to ask if I can help them out or even to get work.

When you're starting out, particularly as a puppet-maker, don't be afraid to ask lots of questions to whoever's leading the build – we love questions as they help you to learn, they help us get the puppets made the way we like, and sometimes they help us to question the way we're doing things so we can work towards making the best thing possible. There is also amazing online content nowadays, with makers sharing their processes on social media. If possible, buy what tools and materials you can and have a go at watching and copying these processes at home to start building these skills. Also, if you can afford to do some short courses, consider skills-based courses that might well seem 'outside' of puppet-making but will provide a number of relevant and useful skills. For example, doing a shirt-making course involves using all different kinds of stitching and is a great way to cover a huge number of textile skills in one go.

5 REHEARSALS

The most intensive part of the theatre-making process for the puppet itself is rehearsals, as, due to the full days of activity and repetitive action, they are likely to sustain significant wear or suffer breakages. This is very valuable learning as you discover where the stresses and strains of performance show themselves on the puppet, but it can often feel disheartening if things don't withstand or behave as you anticipated. For this reason it is best to send your puppet into rehearsals unfinished, by this I mean structurally complete and functioning but not with its outermost decorations, costume or paint effects. The outermost layers will bear the brunt of rehearsals and often get worn or damaged, so the later they can be applied the better. It will also mean that you are not having to undo the delicate aesthetic work to undertake any significant repairs and reinforcements to the puppet's internal structure or joints in response to rehearsals. Responding to the needs of rehearsals is the main job of the puppet designer and maker/s at this stage, as often new requirements or changes are asked of the puppet while a specific action or staging of a scene is being determined. Some consistent examples of new requirements from rehearsals are:

- **Dexterity:** the puppet needs to pick an object up without the use of a puppeteer's hand so a magnet is added to the puppet and the correlating prop to enable this.
- **Ergonomics:** the puppeteers may require an additional control point or indeed a change of angle or reinforcement to an existing handle or rod to improve their manipulation and comfort.
- **Props:** the puppet may wear or handle something that will need to be altered to make it more functional for the puppet and puppeteers. Often this is about making a prop lighter, adding a tiny tab or rod for ease of handling, or ensuring a worn item doesn't impede the puppet's movement by having it secured or reinforced.

These changes will need implementing before the specific scene or sequence they're required for is rehearsed again, this gives the puppeteers and performers time to experience and integrate the amendments into their performance until they feel second nature. Once all significant changes or additions to the puppet's structure have been made and the character's action has been determined, the puppet will then be taken out of rehearsals at regular intervals, when it is not being used, for the final finishing stages to be completed. Final finishing can be anything from its outermost paint application, or its hair and costume being added. Often these final finishes are in response or relation to the other design elements that are coming together throughout rehearsals, like costume and wigs, hair and make-up.

In *Pinocchio*, the adult human characters were played by larger than life puppets, to make the actor playing Pinocchio appear toy-sized. The actors who voiced the characters and operated the heads of the giant puppets were dressed to match their puppets. So, until the visual language of the actors' wigs and make-up had been determined by the show's designer Bob Crowley, we kept the puppets unpainted and bald. That way we could find a version of the actor's aesthetic which could be scaled up to match the size of the puppets.

FIGURE 5.1 Painting the Blue Fairy and Geppetto puppets from *Pinocchio*.

We used coconut hair fibres to replicate the clown-like hair tufts on the wig worn by the actor playing the Coachman, and we used acrylic paint mixed with gesso primer on the puppets' faces to resemble the textured, wood grain-like make-up worn by the acting company.

> **FACT**
>
> The National Theatre's Wigs, Hair and Make-up department created a twice life-sized moustache and wig for the Geppetto puppet in *Pinocchio* to ensure an identical match to those worn by actor Mark Hadfield, who voiced the character.

Puppetry director

Whether a puppet has a single puppeteer or multiple operators working in unison, it is during rehearsals that they will become proficient at animating its character in a coordinated and expressive way. This is often done with the help of a puppetry director, a member of the creative team who works in collaboration with the director and sometimes choreographer to ensure that the puppet's movements and actions are as detailed and precise as possible. A puppetry director often refines and rehearses a puppet's actions separately with the puppeteers, after the overall blocking or action of a scene has been set by the wider creative team. Sometimes, if the performers selected to animate the puppet have no puppetry experience, it is the responsibility of the puppetry director to train up these performers with the skills necessary to puppeteer, so rehearsals become a process of the performers not only creating and refining the show, but also learning and developing a very technical new skill from scratch. Regardless of a performer's puppetry experience, the role of a puppeteer has two primary functions:

- **To live (technical task):** before a puppet can start to play its part it has to convince the audience that it is alive, showing that it is every bit as expressive, vulnerable and functional as we are. For the puppeteers, this is about maintaining the basic principles of life and movement (more detail on these later in the chapter) throughout their performance.
- **To act (character task):** in addition to the puppet living and functioning as a 'real' being, the puppet then can undertake the work of an actor, inhabiting its role and playing the motivations and objectives it has throughout the narrative. For the puppeteers, this involves a lot of specificity and care, ensuring no action or movement is extraneous or distracting.

This balancing act of maintaining the technical skill and playing the character can be a very daunting one, but, throughout the days and weeks of rehearsals, it is always very satisfying to see puppeteers become more physically fluent with both their puppet and each other. Resulting in the more technical, fundamental signs of life becoming second nature to perform, and integrating them alongside the puppet's character and onstage actions as they develop. From here the puppet becomes an actor in the rehearsal room in its own right, and often the puppetry director, director and other creative team members will directly address or refer to the puppet instead of giving notes or asking questions to its puppeteers.

Puppeteer principles

The techniques and methodology of bringing a puppet to life are vast and varied, and are often dictated by the style of puppet or the number of performers animating it. There are, however, some excellent core principles that you can apply to any mode of puppetry, as they provide the backbone for an audience's ability to understand and emotionally invest in your puppet. Here are the three most fundamental principles, and how they apply to both the puppet and puppeteer/s.

	For the puppet	For the puppeteer
Breath	Breath is the most fundamental way of showing life in the puppet. it allows the audience to see and understand the puppet's physiological state. Changing the rhythm of breath creates different emotions.	The puppeteer operating the head vocalizes the breath for the puppet. It becomes an invaluable way for teams of puppeteers to listen to each other and synchronize the puppet's thoughts and actions.
Focus	The puppet's eye-line shows its interest in, or intention towards something. Changing the eye-line indicates a new thought or intention.	When a puppeteer's focus remains on their puppet, this encourages the audience to look at the puppet and not at them, rendering them 'invisible'.
Weight	Showing the puppet's weight grounds it in our reality and stops it from being a superhuman or fantastical being. Weight is demonstrated by showing the use of muscles against gravity, e.g. prepping down into your leg muscles before you jump.	Puppeteers should have an efficiency and neutrality in their weight to remain invisible, staying centred and minimizing your own body's extraneous movement stops you from pulling the audience's focus away from the puppet.

Alongside these principles, there are some practical techniques that performers can employ to immerse themselves in the act of puppeteering. The first is to acknowledge that puppetry is often painful, as you may have to adopt uncomfortable positions for the puppet to exist in neutral, or perhaps you'll have to hold your puppet out in front of you for prolonged periods of time. Rehearsals are the time your body will work through such discomfort and develop the stamina needed to perform the character. It then becomes important to realign your body after intensive periods of work (see information on 'warm downs' in Chapter 7). While the physical demands of puppeteering can be specific, it is worth acknowledging that due to the bespoke nature of a puppet's design for a specific production, they can often be tailored to accommodate a performer's additional needs or preferred practice. So, seeing your rehearsal process as a collaboration of both you and the puppet learning how to move in response to each other, and how the work of the puppet designer and makers can help facilitate this. Something else that will develop throughout rehearsals is your peripheral vision, meaning your ability to see and analyse people, objects and activity outside of your direct line of sight. By having to look at their puppet to focus the audience's attention, a puppeteer must rely solely on their periphery to take in all of the other action on stage and register visual cues or other relevant information. It can feel very intimidating or debilitating at first, but eventually your awareness will expand and find both confidence and control.

If you're working in a team of puppeteers, then keeping a very slight tension in the limbs and body of the puppet between you all will help each puppeteer feel and respond to each other's offers through the puppet more directly. For example, a puppeteer on the feet of a character will feel the slight pull of intention from the chest and head wanting to move forward far more quickly if the two body parts are in tension, rather than having slack between them that will delay the physical signals.

FIGURE 5.2 Joe Idris-Roberts as Pinocchio, with Audrey Brisson and James Charlton as Jiminy Cricket in *Pinocchio* rehearsals.

In addition to implementing principles and techniques to animate their puppet, a puppeteer also has another ongoing task throughout rehearsals, which is to create what I refer to as a 'physical script' for the puppet's actions. A script traditionally comprises the spoken text for the show, alongside occasional stage directions for the performers. Throughout rehearsals it is an actor's job to annotate their blocking in a scene and the thoughts and actions that instigate it. However, a puppet, whether it has spoken lines of dialogue or not, will very often have specific physical reactions or cues within a scene that are in response or relate to the other characters on stage. These are subtle, physical movements that have the same impact as a spoken line of text and shouldn't be spoken over or distracted from as they allow the audience to read and imprint on the puppet's emotions. It is important for these actions and the thoughts that instigate them to be documented and registered as a team, as this consolidates the story beats for the puppet and forms the 'physical script' of notes and blocking action alongside the existing text and stage directions in the script. These beats are also invaluable if there is a team of puppeteers operating one character, as it helps to align the thoughts and broader gestures of the character, it may well be used by the creative and stage management teams if a puppet's specific movement or reaction is cue for another element on stage, like lighting and sound.

> **TIP**
>
> When puppeteering, try not to use mirrors as a means of seeing what the puppet looks like to the audience, as your focus will be sent out to the reflection and you won't gain a sense of what movements look and feel like from the inside. Instead, ask a colleague to film the action and analyse it during playback.

Interview with Audrey Brisson

Audrey Brisson is an Olivier-nominated actress who started her career working with Cirque du Soleil, both as a vocalist and an acrobat. In 2017, she originated the role of Jiminy Cricket in *Pinocchio* at the National Theatre.

TO Before Jiminy Cricket, did you have any experience performing with puppets?

AB My first experience with puppets was in Kneehigh's *The Wild Bride*, in which I operated a small bird and a beautiful wooden girl. I remember finding such peace when manipulating the puppets, as if they had a life of their own, and that my job was to listen and respond to what they wanted to do. Each puppet has its own personality, a rhythm they prefer, movements they resist, etc. These puppets were of the mythical world, made of branches and leaves, therefore my manipulation needed to feel as delicate as wind moving through a tree. I then played Dea in *The Grinning Man* at the Bristol Old Vic, where I puppeteered the younger version of my character in flashbacks. It was exciting to capture her youth and energy using a puppet instead of playing her as a child myself. It allowed for a clarity of thought and emotion, trusting that the scale and appearance of the puppet would be endearing to the audience and emanate innocence enough without having to oversimplify the character, which can often happen when adults play children on stage.

TO What were your initial thoughts about performing a character solely as a puppet?

AB When I found out I would be playing Jiminy Cricket I remember feeling immense joy and excitement, but mixed with trepidation and fear that I wouldn't be up to the challenge. Working alongside James Charlton who puppeteered Jiminy's feet, it was important to me that beyond the comedy and largeness of her as a character, I wanted the audience to be able to feel Jiminy's sensitivity and truth. I didn't want her to simply live in broad strokes and I didn't know if the little experience that I had as a puppeteer would be enough.

TO How did your puppetry skills develop throughout rehearsals?

AB When we started *Pinocchio* rehearsals, I found it very physically challenging. Jiminy was not a heavy puppet, and yet holding her for an entire scene felt like an impossible task. I remember being extremely worried that I wouldn't be able to deliver and perform her for the length of the entire show. Then one day, halfway through the rehearsal process, James and I, as Jiminy, were asked to host a group of children who had come to watch some extracts of rehearsals. Suddenly we weren't performing a scene with existing movements and words, we were chatting with the kids, responding to them, being in the moment and improvising, Jiminy even led a warm-up for the group. It wasn't until the end of the session that I realized my arms didn't feel tired and that I had not only managed to survive, I had felt free. Jiminy had come to life, she was no longer restricted by the tension in my body. I wasn't over-gripping the puppet any more, holding on for dear life in a worried state. I realized just how important it is to see the puppet as an extension of your arm, rather than an object you're carrying, you are continuing physical thoughts all the way through your arm and into the puppet. And in order for the thought to carry to the extremity, you need to release any tension. I was surprised how much I could relax my hands and muscles as a puppeteer without actually dropping the puppet after that.

From then it never felt like I was holding Jiminy, I was supporting her, helping her come to life. What had also emerged during Jiminy's long improvisation was the silent 'conversation' between myself and James while puppeteering. We were suddenly starting to understand one another's body language and were able to respond to each other's physical 'offers' through the puppet. James could feel if I wanted to move left or right, or if Jiminy needed to compress or jump, and similarly I was able to respond and react to his offers of Jiminy's insect-like twitches or worried stamping. We had become a team. Yes, I might have spoken the words, but Jiminy was both James and me.

TO What are the differences between performing as an actor and performing through a puppet?

AB Actors and puppeteers have the same job, that of being a storyteller. However, a puppeteer's energy is sent towards their puppet, whereas an actor's energy isn't channelled anywhere else, it is in you to then send directly to the audience.

Aside from the placement of energy, I don't think there's actually much difference between performing as an actor and performing through a puppet. Many of the same rules apply; those of focus, listening to your fellow performers and clarity of thoughts. It is perhaps simply less forgiving for a puppet than it is for human actors. If an actor's energy on stage is unfocused and all over the place, the audience may have an opinion as to the quality of the performance, but they still believe the actor to be real. Therefore, the leap to then believing in the character is somewhat smaller than, for instance, if a puppet seems to be similarly looking everywhere and nowhere, then the audience stops believing it to be alive. They see the puppet as a manipulated object and not a living character. As a puppeteer it is your job to help the audience suspend their disbelief and make them see a character via the puppet, not you.

TO Have you found your process as an actor has changed since working as a puppeteer?

AB Working with puppets has strengthened my appreciation of the economy of an actor's movement on stage. Working with puppets, you discover quickly how unnecessary movements lessen the clarity of thought. If your puppet is moving aimlessly while talking and looking everywhere and nowhere, the audience struggles to understand what the puppet is saying and or thinking, making it easy for their brain to switch off and stop believing in its life. But by embracing stillness, combined with movements that have a clear beginning and end (just like a sentence), you help to focus both the audience's attention and their understanding of the scene. Who are they looking at, who is speaking, what are they thinking, who is speaking as a result, etc. It's just like a game of ping pong! And so, just like a puppet, your own body as an actor is an extension of your thoughts and feelings. By stripping down all the unnecessary tension and movement you find clarity in performing only what is essential and therefore most expressive.

6 TECHNICAL REHEARSALS

Technical rehearsals or 'tech' are where the cast and creative team move from the rehearsal room onto the stage and work through the entire show from start to finish, adding all of the remaining elements that weren't present in the rehearsals, like lighting, sound and automation, while also getting to see and work with finished elements like scenery, costumes, wigs and props for the first time. This is a perfect opportunity to see the finished puppet in the context of all the other design elements on stage that it will be interacting with or even seen against. Tech also gives you the chance to see how the puppet reads from the audience's perspective in the auditorium, as they are probably going to be viewing the action from further away than you did in the rehearsal room. There are two common situations that occur when looking at your puppet during technical rehearsals

- **Loss of detail:** some paint effects, patterns or finishes, even the style of eye and pupil, may not read as clearly from further away. Often this means increasing the contrast between colours, shading or textures, or making patterns larger or bolder. A puppet could be made so that its eyes can be swapped out in tech until the ideal option is found.

- **Reduced visibility:** the puppet and its actions aren't as clear as hoped, perhaps because the puppeteers are too present. This can often be remedied by increasing the contrast between the puppet and its operators, using either the puppet's colour, the puppeteer's costume or tighter lighting.

During technical rehearsals for *Pinocchio*, the puppetry department suffered a major setback when we first saw Jiminy Cricket on stage for the first time. We had sent the puppet to a company that painted cars and motorbikes, as we wanted to use an exciting kind of colour shifting iridescent paint that required a very long, labour-intensive (and expensive) process traditionally used when customizing vehicles. When the Jiminy Cricket puppet arrived back it looked incredible, with an insect-like shimmer to its finish that flashed between green and purple under the halogen lights of the National Theatre's props workshop. Yet when the moment of truth came and we saw the puppet on stage under stage lighting it looked black, with none of its shimmering colour or indeed its overall shape visible to the audience. Suddenly, Audrey and James, Jiminy's puppeteers, were more visible and present than their puppet. So, we had no choice but to

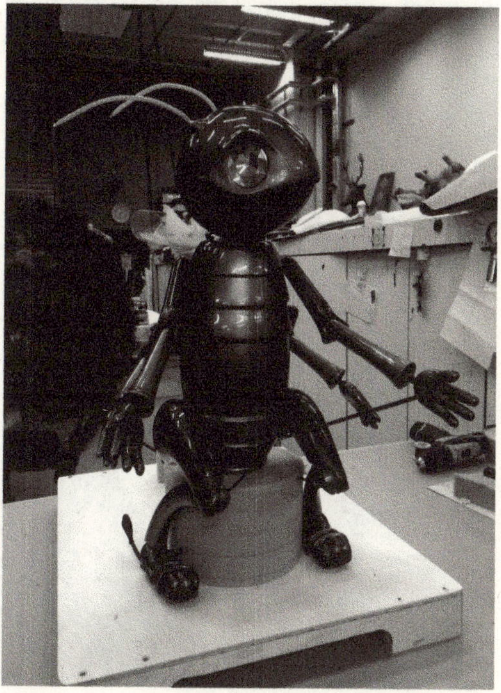

FIGURE 6.1 The colour-shifting paint finish on the completed Jiminy Cricket puppet.

completely rethink and overhaul the aesthetic of Jiminy with less than a week to go before performances started.

I sat in the auditorium with my sketchbook and reference images of garish insects to design a bolder colour palette,

FIGURE 6.2 Jiminy Cricket's revised paint finish being applied.

and Daisy Beattie the puppet supervisor, worked with Lara Scott from the props department to carefully sand away the beautiful but unsuccessful paint finish. In the end, Jiminy Cricket was a very luminous lime green, with warm yellow highlights on all of her joints and limbs to emphasize her movements. Although it was a stressful, unexpected hurdle, I learnt that you should never take for granted how something looks up close compared to how it appears on stage.

Puppeteer stamina

Technical rehearsals are a very exhausting part of the process for everybody on stage, backstage and in the creative team. You work long hours for several days in a row, often waiting while technical elements are adjusted or determined, and repeating transitions or trickier bits of staging until they are perfect. Because puppetry is a very physical job, often requiring the puppeteers to be in unusual positions and postures, it is important in tech to acknowledge when the puppet's performance can be marked or walked through, and when it requires full performance energy and intensity, as this will avoid any unnecessary strain or fatigue on the puppeteers' bodies and muscles during the prolonged, repetitive work of tech. It also ensures that once technical rehearsals are over and a dress rehearsal gets underway the puppeteers are able to perform to the best of their abilities. Throughout rehearsals, puppeteers may have used protective and preventive measures like gloves or knee pads to avoid any pain or discomfort caused by repetitive gripping or kneeling. If the performer has decided that these are necessary for the duration of the run, then it is during tech that these elements are refined and integrated, either by being hidden or dressed to match the outer aesthetic and palette of their costume.

> **TIP**
>
> Wearing gloves while puppeteering is a great way to avoid any friction or bruising to your hands. However, sometimes they can reduce grip, so it is best to opt for gloves used in activities like cycling or weight lifting as they often have panels of grip texture in the palm and are mostly fingerless, which helps to maintain dexterity.

Puppet technician

If the puppets on a production are particularly intricate or numerous, very often a puppet technician is employed to coordinate, repair and maintain them during a production's run. This technician usually joins the process during rehearsals, where they work alongside the stage management team to create tracking plots for the puppets and note where they move and need to be placed backstage in relation to their action on stage. In tech and during performances, the puppet technician works backstage in a puppetry specific 'track', meaning a route where they are moving around to watch the puppet's actions on stage and are prepared to repair any breakages mid-show. During the performance they might also have cues where they pre-set, receive and hand off puppets to the performers, and perform any costume or aesthetic changes that need to occur between a puppet's scenes. Puppet technicians are generally either people who have trained in stage management and have experience in making and repairing props, or people who have started out as puppet-makers, but have the communication and organizational skills to work as part of the backstage team and work under pressure.

I often compare puppets to musical instruments instead of props, as they must be handled from specific places, often need readjusting during a performance and require stands or hanging points backstage to ensure they're safe. So, in this example, the puppet technician is the equivalent of a piano tuner, someone who knows how the equipment functions and when it is performing at its best, and has the expertise to identify and remedy any problems.

TIP

The speed or haste with which a puppet is picked up or put back into its storage area backstage during a performance can sometimes cause minor damage like scuffs or dents. To avoid this, cover any contact or resting points of the puppet storage racks or stands in soft materials such as scraps of foam or serge fabric.

FACT

During both the original 2007 run and 2008 revival of *War Horse* at the National Theatre, each puppet had its own portable 'stable' backstage. These wheeled frames had clipping points that the puppets were suspended from, allowing stage management to move the life-sized horses easily around between scenes.

7 IN PERFORMANCE

Once a production has officially opened, the work of the puppet designer and puppet-makers is complete, but for the other disciplines the ongoing run of performances requires a number of processes to preserve the quality, care and maintenance of both the puppeteers' and puppets' performance.

Puppeteers

For those involved in the performance on stage it is important to maintain their body's strength, flexibility and stamina throughout the run. Particularly as sustained postures and repetitive actions can create strain and injury over time. To avoid such strains over a production's run, it is vital to implement preventative measures rather than rely on reactive treatments in the aftermath of an injury. The most straightforward measures (which should be started as early as day one of rehearsals) are a thorough physical warm-up prior to working and an appropriate warm-down afterwards. But what is the difference between a warm-up and warm-down I hear you ask? Well they will differ depending on the specific activity of a production or the kind of puppets involved, but some helpful starting points are:

Warm-up:

- **Active stretching**: focusing on one specific muscle group to stretch another.
- **Core activation**: building strength to maintain your body in ideal postures.
- **Cardiovascular exercises**: activities to increase your heart rate, breathing and blood flow.

Warm-down:

- **Passive stretching**: using an object, or external force to provide a stretch to a specific muscle group.
- **Nerve flossing**: stretches that can increase your range of motion and relieve pain.
- **Hot and cold treatments**: can help relieve any aching pain caused from muscle or joint over-activity.

In addition to maintaining their bodies, it is also beneficial for puppeteers to nurture and sustain their focus and connection, either between a single puppeteer and their puppet, or between a team of puppeteers operating a single character. Throughout a run, the coordination and symbiosis between puppeteers and their puppets can become so fluent

FIGURE 7.1 Actor Emily Mytton warming-up during rehearsals for *War Horse*.

and precise that the puppet's action might appear like perfectly executed choreography rather than organic, motivated thoughts and reactions. So, it is important for puppeteers to try and maintain a state of active listening, tuning into the variations and imperfections of that performance, rather than anticipating the movements or cues that are coming because that is how they were rehearsed. A simple but playful way of maintaining a state of active listening is taking time between the warm-up and the performance to operate your puppet outside the fixed action of the show. Whether that is improvising as your puppet wanders around the stage and interacts with castmates, or giving the puppet some physical activities it may not undertake in the show. This way, the puppeteers continue to stay tuned into each other in an immediate and live way, using different 'muscles' for the puppet and thinking outside of the show's current context.

EXERCISE: PUPPETRY ASSAULT COURSE

To develop a group of puppeteers' active listening, create an assault course for the puppet from everyday items, like chairs, a table or stacks of boxes. Without any planning or speaking to each other, the puppeteers must navigate their puppet through the terrain (by climbing, jumping, swinging, etc.), problem-solving as they go through the character's thinking and tactics.

Puppetry director

Throughout the run of a production the puppetry director may be on retainer or have a contractual responsibility to watch the show at regular intervals, and give notes to the puppeteers on their performance. These notes can be as simple as maintaining blocking or checking cues, but often there is a responsibility to help preserve the clarity of the puppet's performance throughout the run. Over time, the story beats within a puppet's physical action can blur or distort, making it harder for an audience to read and interpret. Some of the most common outcomes that can cause this are:

- **Increase in speed:** the strength and fluidity of the puppeteers may have developed so much that an action or movement sequence has become so fast its meaning is hard to decipher. Or, perhaps the movement is finishing too early in relation to a sound or lighting cue, resulting in a pause or other elements on stage having to compensate.
- **Lack of stillness:** the pauses and stillness that a puppet uses to allow the audience to interpret its prior gestures and expressions get filled with new thoughts or extra actions. This results in a very busy or hyperactive train of thought for the puppet that may well pull focus from other characters and action on stage, or muddy the puppet's intentions for the audience.
- **Synchronizing rhythms:** through the repetition of the performance, puppeteers and their puppets may well start to adopt each other's rhythms or perhaps the rhythms of other characters on stage. This can lead to a lack of contrast or variation in movement, resulting in the puppet's motion becoming repetitive, overly synchronized and inorganic.

Rather than tackling these habits technically or choreographically, often the most effective way to reinstate clarity is to encourage the puppeteers to check back in on the character's objectives, intentions and impulses. Re-establishing the puppet's thoughts and internal narrative will inform the action it takes, and as a result often opens up a bit more air time in the action and consolidates the character's presence and activity in the narrative. The most satisfying part of being a puppetry director is seeing the puppeteer's work grow and develop over the course of run, not by them adding new moves or material, but by deepening and enriching the character and their relationship to it.

On a long-running show, where the physical demands of a production are very intense for the puppeteers, the puppetry director will often create a rotation system to ensure their bodies don't undergo any excess strain throughout the run. This can have many forms, including: puppeteers working in a team rotating through the different parts of their character,

FACT

The rotation system of *War Horse* puppeteers combines the three puppeteers of Joey as a foal moving between the head, heart and hind positions, as well as four teams of three puppeteers who alternate between playing adult Joey and Topthorn.

or whole teams regularly swapping out into a less physically demanding role in the show while an alternate or understudy team plays the part. This kind of rotation and regular rest is a helpful and immediate way of avoiding injuries or intense fatigue that may lead to accidents or bad postural habits.

Puppet supervisor and technician

Once the show is open, the work on the puppets continues, mainly in their ongoing maintenance and documentation. The puppet supervisor will create a 'bible' for the puppets, this is an information pack that outlines the materials used in their construction and any specific suppliers or techniques employed in the process. It may also include a breakdown of the puppet's dimensions and any patterns that were created during construction in case duplicate puppets might need to be made in the future without access to the originals.

One such example of this is making understudy puppets. If a character is deemed 'story essential', meaning that the show can't continue without them, a replica or replacement parts are often made to ensure the performance can continue if a severe break occurs. For *Pinocchio* we made a duplicate Jiminy Cricket puppet, as she was a central character in the story and it was such a physical track – thankfully, due to the fact we used moulds to make her this was a much swifter

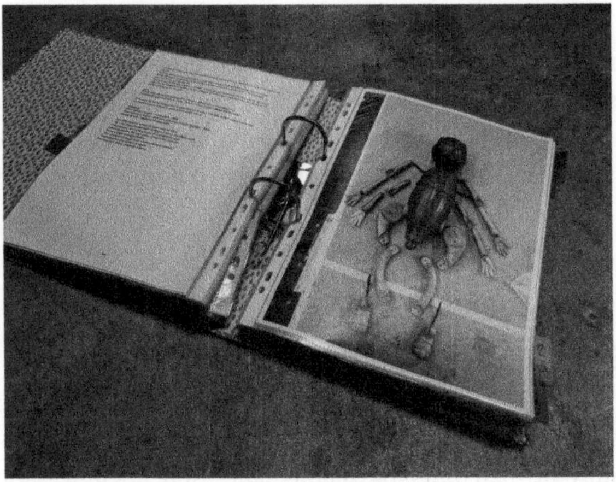

FIGURE 7.2 The puppetry bible made by puppet supervisor Daisy Beattie for *Pinocchio*.

process than starting from scratch. In contrast, *War Horse* only had duplicate heads and legs of the horses made, as these were more intricate and vulnerable than its body, so a simple limb swap pit-stop could be employed mid-show if a breakage occurred.

The puppet technician is the person responsible for remedying such mid-show breaks, which thankfully are rare, mainly because the puppet technician themself has weekly maintenance hours on the puppets between shows to repair and anticipate any wear and tear. Some elements of a puppet may need regular maintenance and replacement,

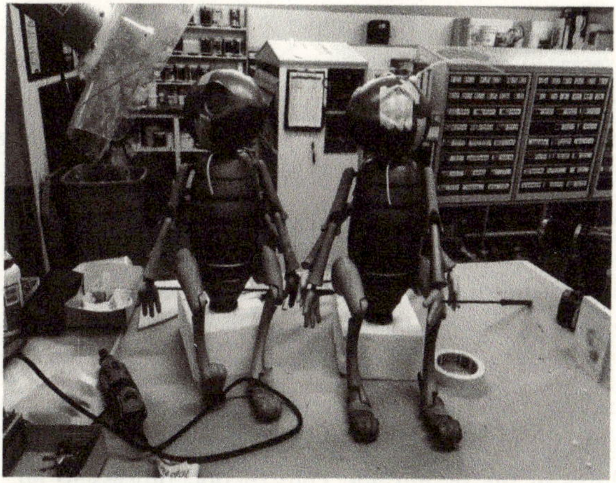

FIGURE 7.3 Replica Jiminy Cricket puppets under construction.
© Toby Olié, 2017.

whereas others may last the whole run untouched. Here are some examples of the kinds of maintenance a puppet might require due to repeated use:

- Replacing worn elastic bungees or cords.
- Touching up chipped paint and varnish finishing.
- Patching or stitching fabric coverings.
- Upgrading worn hardware like bolts, eyelets or springs.
- Substitute crushed or torn foam for new pieces.
- Cleaning due to dulling or discolouring from handling or contact with the stage floor.

If an element of the puppet is needing constant repair or replacement, then the puppet technician will liaise with the puppet supervisor and puppet designer about finding a sturdier or harder-wearing substitution. These changes will then be logged by the puppet technician in their own documentation of fixes, upgrades and repairs that can be implemented into the supervisor's bible. The hand-made nature of puppets means that keeping track of their construction is invaluable, not only for those continuing to work on the production, or even on a potential replica production, but for the puppet designer and makers as a means of archiving their discoveries, successes and even failures of the design and construction process to enable continued learning and improvement.

CONCLUSION

When I am introduced to someone new, the person doing the introducing will often describe my job as a 'puppet master', which usually makes me wince, mainly because of its connotations of an eccentric old hermit or weird horror movie villain. But after some embarrassed justifications to the person I'm being introduced to, I begrudgingly welcome the all-encompassing job title feeling lucky that my work includes all of the explorative, collaborative, imaginative, distinctive challenges and joys of working in puppetry.

If the creation or performance of a puppet looks and feels organic or effortless, often a director or producer will assume that it was quick or easy to accomplish, which, as you have just read, is far from the case. Therefore, the combination of skills, time and dedication that goes into puppetry can easily be undervalued, so as an artist you consistently find yourself having to stand your ground on how much money or time things will take to create. But championing the unique abilities of puppetry, and what its potential can be with the right support is often the best way to enlighten and galvanize the collaborators and institutions who will help you do your best work. As a freelance artist working in a relatively niche discipline, you can be made to feel that being in paid employment is a privilege and so making requests for adjustments to your salary, crediting, responsibilities or contribution to the work is ungrateful or obstructive. In these instances, I would say it is very helpful to have confidence in your own worth and think about how an audience's experience of the production would differ without your contribution in it. If the difference is significant and you're being undervalued, then as daunting as it might seem, saying 'No' can be a very empowering thing.

With the increased use and appreciation of puppetry in theatre over the past few decades, both audiences' palates for and expectations of the artform are deepening and broadening. As a result, productions are able to be bolder and more experimental in their use of puppets and puppeteers therein. This brings a new set of rewards and challenges for puppetry, particularly with regards to environmental impact, as often the most lightweight and robust materials used in puppet-making are the least environmentally friendly. So, myself and many other artists are experimenting and implementing strategies to reduce and streamline the use of such materials with the hope that one day we may be able to cease using them completely. These strategies take many forms, from prioritizing adhesives and glazes that don't include hazardous or harmful chemical components, to finding substitutes for less sustainable raw materials. For example, Piñatex is a material that is made from fibres extracted from pineapple leaves and works perfectly as an entirely animal-cruelty-free alternative to leather.

For such an ancient, hand-made performance medium to still be evoking and entertaining audiences, particularly at this time of rapid technological innovation, is very encouraging. It demonstrates that puppetry will continue to thrive as long as those that create it keep challenging themselves and invigorating the art form. Not only as a means of longevity, but increasing its abilities to cross generational boundaries and language barriers to be as inclusive as possible, and inspire many more generations to come.

Interview with Sarah Wright

Sarah Wright is a puppeteer, director and founder of the Curious School of Puppetry. Her work includes collaborations with Kneehigh, Royal Shakespeare Company, Young Vic, Shakespeare's Globe and Improbable. In 1961, Sarah's parents founded the Little Angel Theatre, where she was a member of the company until 2001.

TO How does puppetry as a discipline fit into theatre-making as a whole?

SW For me 'puppetry' means our interaction with, or the movement of, materials and objects. It means the animation of anything outside of ourselves. It means humans and materials working together to create meaning-making and storytelling through design and manipulation. So, puppetry is everywhere: in visual theatre, dance, animation, and devised and physical theatre. Puppetry is widely used and audiences are becoming very aware of this. Puppetry can be used brilliantly to represent humans or animals on stage, imitating a living being with realistic movement – but it can be even more exciting to think about puppetry in more abstract ways – animating materials and objects to create atmospheres, dreams and landscapes. Or working with non-literal scales, for example using changes in scale to show shifting power dynamics. This more abstract use of puppetry can be a powerful tool in sharing non-verbal experiences with an audience.

TO What are the challenges and opportunities for the industry right now?

SW Audiences are responding so positively to puppetry – these audiences provide a wonderful opportunity for theatre-makers to expand their skills and explore the many varied ways puppetry can be used. The challenge is to find partners; venues and backers or funders, that will support this experimentation and provide space to try new visual ways of working. It is wonderful that so many loved books and films are being adapted for the stage with puppetry.

But the challenge is to create new ideas, where design and performance are brought together in imaginative forms.

TO How can puppetry support a greater diversity of makers and performers in productions?

SW Puppetry can support greater diversity by opening up routes of access to this form of theatre-making. Puppetry has traditionally been a rather closed scene. In many parts of the world, including the UK, puppetry was traditionally passed down within families. Shows were built and performed by couples touring together or by small companies who trained their own communities, or sometimes in an amateur way, just for fun. I grew up at the Little Angel Theatre, at a time where there were no training opportunities, we learnt to make and perform puppets as part of a full-time 'resident company'. It's been very important within my working life to open the form, find points of shared knowledge with other forms of theatre and art, and to broaden the reach to artists and audiences alike. By starting the Curious School of Puppetry I wanted to offer a reliable pathway to becoming a professional puppeteer that is widely accessible.

TO What are the top three skills you think someone working in puppetry needs?

SW Focus: undoubtedly an ability to focus on your puppet or materials, to quieten yourself in order to work through a figure, to give your full attention to it. I believe an audience can tell when a performer's attention is not wholly present. This may sound obvious, but we are so easily distracted by others, by our phones, by thinking 'is this any good?' that it can be difficult to really listen and let a puppet lead us.

Collaboration: is absolutely key. Whether that is collaboration with others in the rehearsal room, with artists from varied disciplines, or with operators of other limbs of the puppet. There are some amazing solo puppeteers but they are few, and puppetry does not survive egos without a fight, so listening to each other and to the materials is vital in puppetry.

Rhythm: a sense of timing, speed and breath. We can constantly learn more about the usefulness of stillness. It's possible to train ourselves in this by watching silent movies, physical comedy or dance, to see how we collectively understand what is being said without the use of words. Of course words can be used too, but puppetry is primarily a visual form, and because puppets don't always have moving facial features, we find ways to express emotion and story through the rhythm of their physical presence.

TO What are your hopes for the future of puppetry?

SW I hope puppetry will keep evolving, that traditional forms will not be forgotten and that we will continue to witness shows, entirely puppetry perhaps, that are daring and groundbreaking. I hope all aspects of puppetry – the designing, making and performing – will be recognized collectively as a unique art form. And that a national centre for puppetry, perhaps housing the Curious School of Puppetry, will be an inevitable outcome of this.

GLOSSARY

Aesthetic The visual quality of a puppet's outermost design.

Anatomical drawing Artwork depicting the bodily form and structure of a puppet.

Bible Reference documentation of a puppet's structure, construction and finish.

Blueprint A design plan or technical drawing.

Brown paper A robust type of paper made from unbleached wood pulp.

Conceptual drawing Artwork depicting the visual ideas and aesthetic of a puppet.

Dexterity Skill and ease in physical activity relating to the use of hands.

Director A person who leads and supervises the actors and staff in the creation of a piece of theatre.

Dress rehearsal The final run-through of a performance on stage prior to public performances.

Durability The ability to withstand wear, pressure or damage.

Ergonomics Designing and arranging an object so that it can be used efficiently and safely.

Flexbond A water-based flexible adhesive that bonds materials, such as fabrics, plastics, foams and wood.

Freelance Someone who is self-employed and hired to work for different companies on particular activities.

Maquette A small, preliminary model of a larger piece of work.

Mechanism A system of parts working together to create movement.

Mould A hollow form used to give shape to molten or hot liquid material when it cools and hardens.

Papier mâché Layers of paper and glue that become hard when dry,

Performer A person telling a story on stage, including: actors, singers, dancers and puppeteers.

Plastazote A closed-cell thermoplastic polyethylene foam, usually bought in sheets.

Polystyrene A lightweight, usually white, polymer plastic.

Press night The official opening night of a production, when it is reviewed by the press and critics.

Previews The initial public performances of a production prior to the press night when it is still in development.

Producer A person responsible for the management and financial aspects of making a stage production.

Props An inanimate object used in a theatrical performance that is not part of the set or worn by an actor.

Prototype A first or preliminary version from which other forms are developed.

Puppet An inanimate object that is manipulated in performance to embody life.

Puppet designer A person who creates the overall appearance and specific functions of a puppet.

Puppet-maker A person engaged in the construction and fabrication of a puppet.

Puppet supervisor A person who organizes and supports the construction of puppets before overseeing their integration into rehearsals and on stage.

Puppet technician A person who is responsible for the maintenance and repair of puppets throughout a production's run.

Puppeteer A performer who animates an inanimate object to embody life.

Puppetry director A person on the creative team whose job is to work with the puppeteers to create and refine a puppet's performance.

PVA glue More commonly known as wood or craft glue, an adhesive used for porous materials like wood, paper and fabric.

R&D/Research and development A period of activity that is undertaken by theatres or producers in developing new productions.

Rehearsals The period of activity when a production is created with the cast and creative team.

Replica production A duplicate copy of a production that continues to run elsewhere in the world.

Resin A thick and sticky fluid that hardens permanently when left out in the open air for a certain period of time.

Reticulated foam A lightweight, solid foam with a net-like structure made from porous, open-walled bubbles or 'cells'.

Scrimming Reinforcing a material's surface with a layer of strong, open-weave fabric, secured by adhesive.

Stage management The people who organize all the practical and technical aspects of a production, while supporting the different teams involved in the day-to-day running of a show.

Styrofoam A stronger, denser form of polystyrene suitable for sculpting.

Tech/technical rehearsals The period when a production moves from the rehearsal room to the stage.

Thermoplastic A plastic material that becomes pliable or moldable through heating and solidifies upon cooling.

Understudy A performer or puppet that can cover for another performer or puppet in the event of illness, injury or emergency.

Webbing Strong, closely woven fabric used for making items like straps and belts.

Workshop A period of development time for a new production prior to the start of rehearsals.

ABOUT THE AUTHOR

Toby Olié is a director, designer and puppeteer. He creates productions that are both original and unconventional, expanding audience's expectations of what puppetry is capable of. In 2025 he was Olivier Award nominated for his puppetry designs in *Spirited Away* (London Coliseum).

Work as director includes: *The Bear and the Piano* (Royal Shakespeare Company); *The Enormous Crocodile* (Roald Dahl Story Company); *There's a Bear on My Chair* (Southbank Centre & The Egg); *The Wolves in the Walls* (Little Angel Theatre); *Vivaldi's The Four Seasons: A Reimagining* (Shakespeare's Globe); *The Hartlepool Monkey* (UK tour); *The Elephantom* (National Theatre & West End); *War Horse* (associate puppetry director, West End).

Work as puppetry designer/director includes: *The BFG* (Royal Shakespeare Company); *Spirited Away* (Tokyo, London, Shanghai & Korea); *101 Dalmatians* (Regent's Park Open Air Theatre); *Animal Farm* (UK tour); *Pinocchio, Peter Pan, The Light Princess, Hansel & Gretel* (National Theatre);

The Boy and the Beast, *A Robot in the Garden* (Shiki Theatre Company, Japan); *Running Wild* (Chichester Festival Theatre, Regent's Park Open Air Theatre & UK tour); *The Grinning Man* (Bristol Old Vic & West End); Disney's new staging of *The Little Mermaid* (in the Netherlands, Russia & Japan); *Alice's Adventures in Wonderland* (Royal Ballet); *The Wind in the Willows* (Royal Opera House & West End); *Little Shop of Horrors* (Manchester Royal Exchange); *A Christmas Carol*, *The Lion, the Witch and the Wardrobe*, *The Firework-Maker's Daughter*, *Peter Pan* (Chichester Festival Theatre); *Goodnight Mister Tom* (West End & UK tour).

Work as a puppeteer includes: Hind of Joey in the original production of *War Horse* (National Theatre) before moving to Joey's head for the subsequent West End transfer; *Venus and Adonis* (Royal Shakespeare Company); *Angelo* (Little Angel Theatre).